The Andes

By Molly Aloian

🌲 Crabtree Publishing Company

www.crabtreebooks.com

Crabtree Publishing Company

www.crabtreebooks.com

Author: Molly Aloian
Editor: Adrianna Morganelli
Proofreader: Crystal Sikkens
Indexer: Wendy Scavuzzo
Designer: Katherine Berti
Photo researcher: Katherine Berti
Project coordinator: Kathy Middleton
**Production coordinator &
    prepress technician**: Katherine Berti

Front cover: Built in the 1400s by the Inca
    people, Machu Picchu has become a popular
    tourist attraction in the Andes.

Title page: Mount Fitz Roy is on the border
    of Argentina and Chile. It offers a challenge
    to mountain climbers because of its sheer
    granite faces.

Picture credits:
Samara Parent: p. 5
Shutterstock: cover, p. 1, 4, 6, 7, 8, 9, 10, 11, 12, 14 (middle
    and center), 16, 17, 18, 19 (top), 20, 21, 22, 23, 24, 25 (left),
    26, 27 (bottom), 28 (top and bottom), 29, 30, 31, 32, 33,
    34, 35, 36, 37, 38, 39, 40, 41, 42, 43, 44, 45
Wikimedia Commons: Evanphoto: p. 28 (center); Jialing Gao
    www.peace-on-earth.org: p. 25 (right); Inti: p. 19 (bottom);
    National Geophysical Data Center: p. 14 (map); Javier
    Rubilar: p. 27 (top left); United States Geological Survel:
    p. 13 (tectonic plates)

Library and Archives Canada Cataloguing in Publication

Aloian, Molly
    The Andes / Molly Aloian.

(Mountains around the world)
Includes index.
Issued also in electronic formats.
ISBN 978-0-7787-7560-7 (bound).--ISBN 978-0-7787-7567-6 (pbk.)

    1. Andes--Juvenile literature. 2. Andes Region--Juvenile literature.
I. Title. II. Series: Mountains around the world (St. Catharines, Ont.)

F2212.A46 2011   j918   C2011-905230-X

Library of Congress Cataloging-in-Publication Data

Aloian, Molly.
    The Andes / Molly Aloian.
        p. cm. -- (Mountains around the world)
    Includes index.
    ISBN 978-0-7787-7560-7 (reinforced library binding : alk. paper) -- ISBN 978-
    0-7787-7567-6 (pbk. : alk. paper) -- ISBN 978-1-4271-8841-0 (electronic PDF) --
    ISBN 978-1-4271-9744-3 (electronic HTML)
    1. Natural history--Andes--Juvenile literature. 2. Andes--History--Juvenile
    literature. 3. Andes--Environmental conditions--Juvenile literature. 4.
    Mountain life--Andes--Juvenile literature. I. Title. II. Series.

    QH111.A46 2012
    508.83'242--dc23

                                            2011029829

Crabtree Publishing Company
www.crabtreebooks.com   1-800-387-7650

Printed in Canada/092011/MA20110714

Published in Canada
Crabtree Publishing
616 Welland Ave.
St. Catharines, Ontario
L2M 5V6

Published in the United States
Crabtree Publishing
PMB 59051
350 Fifth Avenue, 59th Floor
New York, New York 10118

Published in the United Kingdom
Crabtree Publishing
Maritime House
Basin Road North, Hove
BN41 1WR

Published in Australia
Crabtree Publishing
3 Charles Street
Coburg North
VIC 3058

CONTENTS

Words that are defined in the glossary are in **bold** type
the first time they appear in the text.

CHAPTER 1

The Andes Mountains

The Andes Mountains are one of the most amazing natural landforms on Earth. Located on the western side of South America, they extend for about 5,500 miles (8,851 km) from north to south. They are the longest mountains on Earth! The natural beauty and abundant wildlife of the Andes Mountains have fascinated human beings for thousands of years.

The Andes Mountains run through seven South American countries—Venezuela, Colombia, Ecuador, Peru, Bolivia, Chile, and Argentina.

In the Beginning

The Andes Mountains are millions of years old. They began to form more than 100 million years ago when part of Earth's **crust** under South America collided with part of the crust under the eastern side of the Pacific Ocean. The edges of the crusts crumbled and folded similar to how a piece of paper folds when its edges are pushed together. Over millions of years, the edges were very slowly pushed upward into tall mountains. Most of Earth's largest mountain ranges, including the Himalayas and the Alps, were formed in this way. This common type of mountain is sometimes called a fold mountain.

What is a Mountain?

A mountain is a gigantic natural landform that rises above Earth's surface. A mountain often has steep sides rising to a summit, which is the highest point or peak. Mountains are usually found in long ranges or groups of ranges called chains. They are formed in different ways, but most of the mountains on Earth have formed over millions of years. You may not be able to notice or feel it, but mountains are forming even as you read this book!

Sacred Mountains

Ancient **civilizations** often believed that mountains were **sacred**. For example, ancient Japanese civilizations regarded Mount Fuji as sacred and ancient African civilizations regarded Mount Kenya as sacred. The ancient Greeks believed that their gods lived at the top of Mount Olympus in northern Greece. Some of the peaks of the Andes are sacred to the people living in South America.

Andean peoples believe that certain mountains are sacred because of their solitude and beauty. Worship of the mountains, such as Ausangate, is widespread.

NOTABLE QUOTE

"I was born in the Andes, in the colonial city of Cuenca, Ecuador. The mountains have been my lifelong companions, and I still make my home at their feet. To those of us who are their children, they are alive. We listen to them, learn to read their moods, and respect their power. Sometimes they welcome us with their solid embrace. Other times they shake with fury, and we know to stay away. Still sacred to some, they speak to the souls of all, reminding us how vulnerable we are."

—Pablo Corral Vega, *National Geographic Magazine*

Impact on Earth

Over time, the Andes have impacted Earth in a number of ways. They affect the **climate** over a huge area, including wind, rain, and temperature. They also control the flow of rivers and the water supply to many areas on the continent of South America. The Andes are home to some of Earth's largest volcanoes, and in the far south along the coast of Chile, large glaciers and ice sheets are common.

FAST FACT

The islands of Aruba, Bonaire, and Curaçao are located in the Caribbean Sea, off the coast of Venezuela. You might be surprised to learn that these islands are the submerged peaks of the extreme northern edge of the Andes Mountains.

According to a report by Peru's National Meteorology and Hydrology Service, glaciers in the Andes have lost 20 percent of their volume since 1970.

Tough Stuff

The plants and animals that live in the Andes Mountains are **adapted** to living in harsh mountain conditions. There are thousands of species of tough flowering plants in the Andes. Different types of trees grow at different **elevations**. However, no trees can grow above the tree line because the conditions are simply too cold and windy. Animals including vicuña, guanacos, cougars, foxes, Andean condors, and thousands of other birds are found throughout the Andes. Their bodies have adapted to the climate and the rugged terrain. For example, the vicuña's long, dense, soft fur provides excellent **insulation** against the fluctuating temperatures in the Andes. The vicuña also has thin, firm hooves to help it move across the stony ground of the Andean plateaus.

The vicuña comes down from the hills during the day to feed on grasses and other plants, and then returns to the hills to sleep.

The Andean condor is a type of vulture.

FAST FACT

Within the Andes, there is a variety of other landforms and **eco-regions** including foothills, plains, rain forests, **plateaus**, and deserts.

Tree line

The Polylepis tarapacana has adapted to the cold climate of the Andes mountains. It lives at the highest elevation than any other tree in the world.

From afar, the tree line appears to be a well-defined area, but the trees grow shorter as they approach the tree line until they gradually stop growing.

People in the Andes

Ancient civilizations lived in the Andes for thousands of years before Europeans settled in the area. The Inca had an enormous **empire** that began around 1200 A.D. They were mainly farmers. They built their homes out of stone or adobe. Adobe is a sun-dried mixture of earth and straw, often shaped like bricks. They had advanced **irrigation systems**, and vast networks of roads, palaces, and temples. The remains of these structures can still be seen throughout the Andes.

The prehistoric city of Tiwanaku, located 45 miles (72 km) from La Paz, dominated a large portion of the southern Andes before the powerful Inca empire. Many of the Tiwanaku ruins are still standing today, and are in protected areas to preserve their history.

Spanish Exploration

European explorers and **colonists** arrived in the Andes in the early 1500s. Early Spanish exploration of the mountains consisted of aggressive and violent **raids** on **indigenous** mountain communities. In the process, however, most of the major modern cities in the Andes Mountains were founded, including Bogota, which is the capital of Columbia, and La Paz, which is the capital of Bolivia.

Bogota is the largest city in Colombia. It has many universities and libraries.

The ancient Inca city
of Machu Picchu was
discovered in 1911.

CHAPTER 2

How Did the Andes Form?

The forces of **plate tectonics** are responsible for the formation of the Andes Mountains. The Andes began forming approximately 100 million years ago. The mountain range formed at a subduction zone, which is a boundary where two or more tectonic plates collide.

A large number of active volcanoes form some of the highest peaks in the Andes. For example, the Altiplano, or high plain, is made up of large quantities of ash produced by these volcanoes.

Earth's Layers

Earth is made up of different layers of rock. The outermost layer of Earth is called the crust. Below the crust is the mantle, which is a very thick, dense layer of rock. The mantle is approximately 1,800 miles (2,897 km) thick—much thicker than the crust. The outer core is the next layer. The temperature of the outer core is very hot, but the inner core is even hotter. The temperature of the inner core is about 9,000°F (4,982°C).

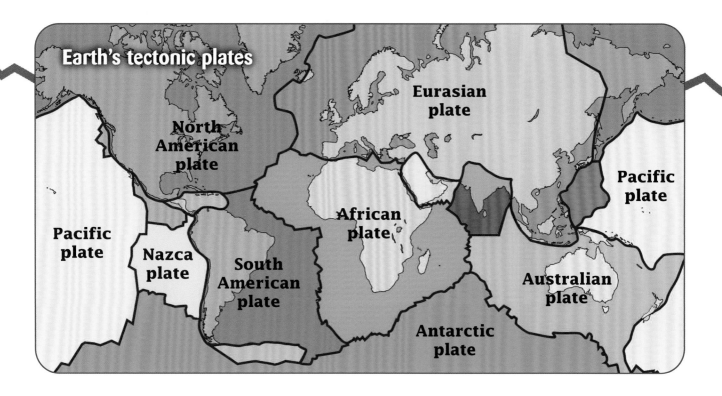

Earth's tectonic plates

North American plate

Eurasian plate

Pacific plate

Pacific plate

African plate

Nazca plate

South American plate

Australian plate

Antarctic plate

Big Changes

The Earth's crust is divided into giant slabs of rock called tectonic plates. These plates do not stay in the same place. They are constantly moving, which causes earthquakes and volcanic eruptions on Earth. They move very slowly, but the changes on Earth can be enormous. As they slowly move, the plates sometimes push up against one another. This causes their edges to slowly force up into gigantic folds and wrinkles—what we know as mountains. The Andes Mountains were formed in this way. However, in order to completely understand the process we must go back in time hundreds of millions of years.

The Nazca Plate

Approximately 200 million years ago, a tectonic plate in the Pacific Ocean, called the Nazca plate, collided with the continental South American plate. The Nazca plate is named after the Nazca region of southern Peru. The Nazca plate began to slide under the South American plate, which is called subduction. It moved only a few inches per year. This slow movement built the Andes over the course of about 75 million years. The plate collision is still occurring today at a rate of about 3.1 to 3.9 inches (8–10 cm) per year.

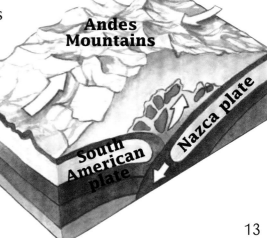

Andes Mountains

Nazca plate

South American plate

Mountain-building

Volcanoes have also helped build the Andes. During volcanic eruptions, hot **lava** was spewed out of volcanoes and cooled to form solid rock. Over millions of years, the rock piled up and built land. Eventually, enough volcanic rock forms a mountain. There are dozens of volcanoes in the Andes that are still building mountains.

This image shows the eruption of the Tungurahua volcano in Ecuador.

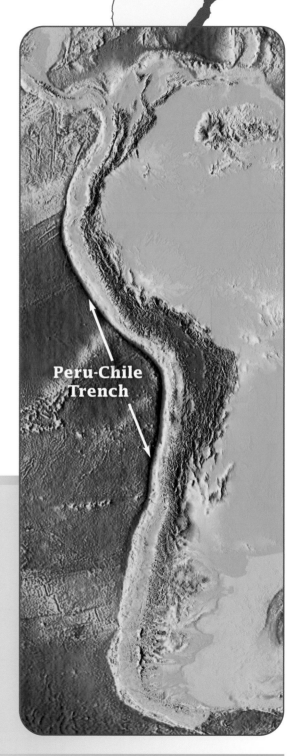

Peru-Chile Trench

FAST FACT
The formation of mountains is called orogenesis.

The Peru-Chile Trench

The Peru-Chile Trench is a long, narrow **depression** in the ocean floor. It marks the subduction of the Nazca plate under the South American plate. The oceanic plate formed this huge trench as it slid underneath the continental plate. The lighter continental plate rose upward into a mountain range. The Peru-Chile Trench reaches a maximum depth of 26,460 feet (8,065 m) below sea level and is approximately 3,666 miles (5,990 km) long.

Many peaks in the Andes rise more than 20,000 feet (6,096 m). The highest peak in the Andes is Aconcagua, which rises 22,834 feet (6,960 m) in western Argentina. It is the highest peak in the western hemisphere.

FAST FACT

In 1960, 1985, and 2011, the shifting Nazca and South American plates caused terrible earthquakes in Chile, killing thousands of people and leaving many more homeless.

Worn Down

As soon as any mountain forms, rainwater and freezing temperatures slowly wear the mountain down. This is called erosion. Rivers carve deep valleys into rocks. Wind blows soil and small bits of rocks away. When water freezes inside a crack in a mountain rock, it swells and can split the rock apart and break it into smaller pieces. Rockslides, avalanches, and earthquakes also change and wear down mountains.

Ring of Fire

There are hundreds of active volcanoes circling the Pacific Ocean in an area called the Ring of Fire. Dozens of these volcanoes, including Cotopaxi and Chimborazo in Ecuador, El Misti in Peru, and Llullaillaco on the border of Chile and Argentina, are found in the Andes Mountains. On November 13, 1985, there was a terrible volcanic eruption in the Andes. A volcano in Columbia, called Nevado del Ruiz, exploded and killed more than 23,000 people.

Cotopaxi, shown here, is in Quito, Ecuador. It is the second highest summit in South America. It is an active volcano, reaching a height of nearly 20,000 feet (6,096 m).

Osorno volcano is an 8,701-foot (2,652 m) volcano in central Chile. Today, it is considered an extinct volcano. Its upper slopes are almost entirely covered with glaciers. Osorno and three other extinct volcanoes form a semicircle of snow-covered volcanic cones in this region of Chile.

Grinding Glaciers

Between 10,000 and 12,000 years ago, massive sheets of ice called glaciers stretched across much of South America. The weight and pressure of the glaciers ground solid rock into dust. The glaciers also dug out riverbeds, carved valleys, and created flat plains across the land. Parts of the Andes still have permanent glaciers that are slowly moving and grinding down the rock of the mountains.

The Perito Moreno Glacier calved into Lake Argentino, in Argentina. Calving is the sudden breaking away of a mass of ice from a glacier.

NOTABLE QUOTE

"When we reached the crest and looked backwards, a glorious view was presented. The atmosphere so **resplendently** *clear, the sky an intense blue, the profound valleys, the wild broken forms, the heaps of ruins piled up during the lapse of ages, the bright colored rocks, contrasted with the quiet mountains of snow, together produced a scene I never could have imagined."*

—Excerpt from Charles Darwin's *Beagle Diary*

The Andes Divided

Today, the Andes are often considered to be a series of loosely connected mountain ranges with depressions, jagged glaciers, and flat, broad plateaus in between. Many experts divide the Andes into three major mountain ranges. The three main ranges are the Cordillera Occidental, the Cordillera Central, and the Cordillera Oriental. The word cordillera means "great mountain chain" in Spanish.

Cordillera Occidental

The Cordillera Occidental is the western range and runs parallel to the coast of the Pacific Ocean. It is moderately high and reaches an elevation of nearly 13,000 feet (3,962 m) at Mount Paramillo before descending in three smaller ranges into the lowlands of northern Colombia. It consists of a line of 19 volcanoes. Seven of these volcanoes exceed 15,000 feet (4,572 m) in elevation.

Cordillera Central

The Cordillera Central is the highest, but shortest of the three ranges. It stretches out for about 400 miles (643 km). There are several volcanoes in this range including the Nevado del Ruiz, Santa Isabel, Nevado del Huila, and Nevado del Tolima.

Cordillera Oriental

The Cordillera Oriental is the longest and widest range. It separates the Magdalena valley from the Llanos. The Llanos are grasslands in western Venezuela and northeastern Columbia. It is narrow to the south, but then broadens out in the high, unsettled massif of the Sumapaz Uplands, with elevations up to 13,000 feet (3,962 m). The average altitude in the Cordillera Oriental is between 7,900 and 8,900 feet (4,408 to 2,712 m).

Chimborazo is the highest summit in Ecuador. It is located in the Cordillera Occidental of the Andes. The top of Chimborazo is completely covered with glaciers.

The Cocora Valley is located in the Cordillera Central of the Andes. It is part of the Los Nevados National Natural Park. The national tree and symbol of Colombia, the Quindio wax palm, is found in the valley.

Vast, tropical grasslands, called the Llanos, are located in Venezuela in the Cordillera Oriental. These lush grasslands are teeming with wildlife such as capybaras, anacondas, giant otters, and hundreds of species of birds.

CHAPTER 3
Weather in the Andes

The Andes are a massive barrier between the Pacific Ocean and the rest of the continent of South America. This barrier impacts the climate of the entire continent of South America.

The rain forests in Ecuador receive abundant rainfall year round.

Scientists sometimes call the center of the Atacama Desert "absolute desert" because it is the driest place in the world.

Different Climates

The climate in the Andes changes drastically throughout the region. For example, there are tropical rain forests in Ecuador that are just a few miles away from the snowy peak of Cotopaxi. The northern part of the Andes is typically rainy and warm. The west side of the central Andes is extremely dry and includes the Atacama Desert in northern Chile. The eastern part of the central Andes is much wetter. In the south, the western side of the Andes tends to be wet, while the eastern plains of Argentina are in a **rain shadow** and tend to be very dry. Many of the peaks in the Andes receive heavy snowfall and contain glaciers.

Varying Temperatures

The temperatures in the Andes vary from country to country. The temperature is also lower at higher elevations, especially at night. In Colombia, the weather is wet and warm, with an average temperature of about 64°F (17°C). In the deserts of Ecuador, the average temperature is about 68°F (20°C). In Bolivia, the weather tends to be hot with an average temperature of 77°F (25°C). Chile is split up into two different temperature regions; the northern part of Chile has an average temperature of 64°F (17°C), and the southern part has an average temperature of 71°F (21°C). In winter, the temperatures usually average less than 52°F (11°C). Summer temperatures usually average 68°F (20°C).

Precipitation

Precipitation within the Andes Mountains varies widely. In the southern mountain regions, annual precipitation can be more than 20 inches (50 cm). In the north, precipitation decreases considerably and becomes seasonal. Even farther north—on the Altiplano of Bolivia, the Peruvian plateau, and in the valleys of Ecuador and the grasslands of Colombia—rainfall is usually moderate, but the amounts vary a lot. It rains only in very small amounts on the west side of the Cordillera Occidental in Peru, but there is more rainfall in Ecuador and Colombia. On the eastern side of the Cordillera Oriental, rainfall usually is seasonal and heavy.

FAST FACT

The Altiplano is a region of high plateaus in northern Chile and Argentina, western Bolivia, and southern Peru. It is the second largest mountain plateau in the world, after that of Tibet.

A huge cloud brings rain over a valley in Peru.

The varying microclimates in the Andes allows vegetation to grow in the valleys right below snow-capped mountain peaks.

Microclimates

There are a wide variety of microclimates in the Andes. A microclimate is a small, distinctly different climate within a larger area. For example, there are numerous microclimates in Peru. In the low-lying valleys, the climate is **temperate** with an average annual temperature of 64°F (17°C). However, the climate is frigid at the highest elevations, where average annual temperatures are below 32°F (0°C).

Current and Climate

The climate of the Andes is greatly influenced by the Humboldt Current, which is also called the Peru Current. This cold ocean current flows northward from the Antarctic along the western coast of South America from the southern tip of Chile to northern Peru. The chilly air that it brings into the atmosphere makes the coasts of the countries bordering the Pacific Ocean very dry.

Cloud Forests

There are cloud forests in the Andes. Cloud forests are evergreen mountain forests that are frequently covered in clouds or mist. Cooler temperatures on mountain slopes cause the clouds to form. In Central and South America, there are cloud forests found from Panama all the way to northern Argentina. These forests are essential to life both on and below mountains because the trees capture water from clouds that would otherwise never fall to the ground as rain. This water, in turn, makes its way downstream and provides billions of gallons of clean water to cities and towns at lower elevations. These forests are also extremely rich in **biological diversity**. The trees in cloud forests are generally between 50 and 65 feet (15 and 19 m) tall and much shorter and mossier at higher elevations.

Much of the biological diversity found in cloud forests is endemic, which means it can be found nowhere else on Earth. For example, most of the shrubs, orchids, and insect-eating plants found on the Cerro de la Neblina in Venezuela are unique to the mountain's summit.

A glacier stream on the Nevado Mismi mountain in Peru is the most distant source of the Amazon River.

(left) The Andes Mountains are the source of many rivers including the Amazon River and the Pilcomayo River. The Amazon begins in the mountains of Peru and flows nearly 4,000 miles (6,437 km) across Brazil to its mouth at the Atlantic Ocean.

NOTABLE QUOTE

"So far we have described only 20 percent of the species—plants and animals—that live in [cloud forests]…In a small area the size of Machu Picchu, we can find the same plant diversity as on the whole continent of Europe."

—Percy Nuñez, **ethnobiologist** specializing in the plants of southern Peru

CHAPTER 4

Plants and Animals

The Andes Mountains support an enormous variety of plants and animals. Different plants and animals live in different parts of the Andes. Cacti and scruffy grasses live in the desert regions while the rain forests are teeming with insects, hummingbirds, frogs, monkeys, as well as flowering plants such as orchids and bromeliads.

Patagonia

Patagonia (above) is a large, remote desert region in the southern Andes covering approximately 260,000 square miles (673,397 square km). A variety of wildlife, including guanacos, pumas, armadillos, foxes, skunks, eagles, and other birds live among the vast, treeless plains. Few people live in Patagonia, but tourism became an important part of the region's economy in the second half of the 20th century.

Guanacos

Armadillo

Bone Dry

The Atacama Desert is in northern Chile and southern Bolivia. The desert covers an area of about 40,600 square miles (105,154 square km). Many scientists believe that the Atacama Desert is the driest place on Earth! Some parts of the desert have not received rain for over 400 years! Some shrubs and low, coarse plants grow in valleys where underground springs provide very little water. One of the few animals that survive in and around the Atacama Desert is the vizcacha, a member of the rodent family. Vizcachas have fleshy pads on the soles of their feet, which help them move quickly over rocky cliffs.

Certain species of plants have been able to adapt to the extremely dry conditions of the Atacama Desert. In spring, some areas are full of color from blooming flowers.

Vizcachas live on dry, sparsely vegetated rocky cliffs and slopes. They are poor diggers but are agile on the rocks, where they look for grasses, mosses, and lichens.

(above) When taking off from the ground and while in flight, flamingos stretch their long necks and legs straight out.

(left) Tinamous mainly eat seeds and fruit found on the ground. At times, they will also eat insects or worms.

Altiplano Plants and Animals

The Altiplano is another dry region, but it is not as dry as the Atacama. Herds of llamas, alpacas, vicuña, and guanacos live in these vast, high grasslands and feed on ichu grasses. Gray foxes and vizcachas also roam the Altiplano. The algae-rich salt lakes are home to large colonies of all three species of South American flamingos. Lizards, deer, and flightless birds called tinamous also live on the Altiplano.

Andean Condor

The Andean condor is a species of vulture that also lives within the Altiplano. It flies throughout the grasslands searching for **carrion** on which to feed. These birds are the largest birds in South America. Their wings are nearly 10 feet (three m) across. They often feed on dead guanacos and alpacas, but they also visit the coasts to feed on dead marine animals such as seals or fish. In doing so, Andean condors perform an important function. They are a natural cleanup crew. The Andean condor is threatened by overhunting. Many farmers shoot Andean condors because they believe the condors kill their **livestock**.

Unlike many other birds, the Andean condor does not build nests. Instead, it lays its eggs only once every two years among boulders or in caves or holes. These places are harder for other predators to reach and provide their eggs and chicks with more protection.

Polylepis Forests

Forests of polylepis trees grow at or above the tree line in the Andes of Colombia, Ecuador, Peru, Bolivia, and Chile. These trees grow at altitudes of 14,760 feet (4,500 m). They have **pinnate** leaves and reddish, multi-layered, papery bark. When they bloom, the forest canopy turns gold. There are approximately 28 species of polylepis in South America. The tropical polylepis is highly endangered and is slowly disappearing because people are clearing land for **grazing** animals and using the trees for firewood and building material. Today, only 10 percent of Bolivia's original polylepis forests remain.

Wet Rain Forests

The rain forests in the Andes Mountains are extremely wet. Some areas receive more than 200 inches (508 cm) of rain per year. There are so many plants and animals living in these rain forests that scientists have not yet discovered them all! There are tens of thousands of species of insects alone. Howler monkeys, tamarins, and marmosets make their homes in the trees. Bats, birds, snakes, lizards, salamanders, and frogs also live in the rain forests.

Cloud Forest Reserve

The Manu Biosphere Reserve in Peru is one of the most **pristine** areas of cloud forest in South America. There are very few human settlements in the park, and hunting and fishing are not permitted. Tourism is strictly controlled and visitors are only allowed into the park if they are accompanied by a registered guide and with a registered tour operator. The cloud forest is home to an incredible variety of wildlife including spectacled bears, toucans, quetzals, howler monkeys, leaf-cutter ants, and thousands of other insects. Scientists estimate that at least 15 percent of the world's bird species live in the park.

Bromeliads grow on trees, rocks, or walls. The roots of these bromeliads are anchoring them to the wall they are growing on.

Howler monkeys live in trees, grasping branches with their hands and tails at all times. They feed mainly on leaves, fruits, nuts, flowers, and buds.

Jaguars

The jaguar is the largest predator in the Andes Mountains. Male jaguars can grow to be up to nine feet (2.7 m) in length, including their tails, with a shoulder height of 2.6 feet (0.8 m). They can weigh between 220 pounds and 350 pounds (100–159 kg). Jaguars are solitary animals, which means they prefer to hunt and live alone in the Andean rain forests.

They are stalk-and-ambush hunters. They hunt agoutis, tapirs, capybaras, fish, frogs, turtles, and caimans. They will also kill cattle, llamas, and goats. Ranchers and farmers kill jaguars to protect their herds of animals so jaguars are constantly threatened by overhunting. Jaguars hunt mainly at night. They are swift, **agile**, and excellent at climbing trees and mountain cliffs.

The Spectacled Bear

The spectacled bear is the only species of bear that lives in the lush cloud forests of the Andes. These bears have shaggy fur that is black, brown, or sometimes reddish in color. They often have white or yellow fur that encircles their eyes, resembling large eyeglasses. They are extremely agile climbers, and have strong jaws and wide, flat **molars** to chew tough vegetation such as tree bark and orchid bulbs. Scientists estimate that there are fewer than 3,000 spectacled bears living in the wild today. They are threatened by habitat destruction. Poachers also hunt spectacled bears for their meat and body parts, and farmers kill them as **agricultural** pests.

The spectacled bear is robust, with a short and muscular neck. It has short but strong legs, each with five toes armed with curved claws up to two inches (five cm) in length.

Lake Titicaca is the highest lake in the world that is capable of carrying large ships.

Lake Titicaca

Hundreds of species of plants and animals live in and around Lake Titicaca. Lake Titicaca is 12,507 feet (3,812 meters) above sea level. It is between Bolivia and Peru. The lake is home to fish, birds, frogs, and other animals. A reed-like plant called totora grows in the marshy, shallow areas of Lake Titicaca. People use bundles of dried totora to make boats for traveling on the lake. Indigenous people, called the Uru, live on Lake Titicaca on floating islands that are made from totora. Its dense roots support the top layers of the islands, which slowly rot from the water. These top layers must be replaced regularly by stacking more reeds on top of the layer beneath. The islands are part of the Titicaca National Reserve, which was created in 1978 to preserve 37 thousand hectares of Lake Titicaca. Over 60 species of native birds, four families of fish, and 18 native amphibians species are protected by the reserve.

This picture shows a reed island in Lake Titicaca. The homes and other structures on the island are also made from totora. The roofs are waterproof. Fires for cooking are built on a layer of stones to protect the reeds.

CHAPTER 5

People in the Andes Mountains

People have been living in the Andes Mountains for thousands of years. Ancient people were the first to farm the land and hunt the animals in the mountains. Many of the people living in the mountains today are still farmers. People from all over the world visit the Andes to witness their natural beauty and attempt to climb their peaks.

The Andes Mountains have more peaks over 10,000 feet (3,848 m) than any other mountain range on Earth. These high peaks lure mountain climbers to the Andes like a magnet.

Hunting and Gathering

Approximately 20,000 years ago, people called **nomads** entered North America. Many experts believe that these people entered North America from Siberia and traveled into Alaska. Eventually, they reached South America through the Isthmus of Panama. An isthmus is a narrow strip of land with water on either side, forming a link between two larger areas of land. These nomads were hunter-gatherers and they moved from place to place to hunt animals and gather food.

Different Cultures

Over time, different civilizations emerged in the Andes Mountains including the Nazca, the Quitus, and the Tiahuanaco. They built cities and farmed the land. In about 200 B.C., the Nazca people carved hundreds of **geometric** lines and images of birds and other animals in the desert. On the ground, these shapes just look like pathways. They are best viewed from overhead. The shapes were discovered in 1939 by an archaeologist named Paul Kosok.

FAST FACT

Today, more than one million people live in the Atacama Desert. They live mainly in coastal cities, mining compounds, fishing villages, and **oasis** towns. Farmers in the far northern regions of the desert grow olives, tomatoes, and cucumbers with drip-irrigation systems. They gather what little water they can from **aquifers**.

One of the most well-known Nazca shapes is called the Astronaut. It is approximately 105 feet (32 m) long and is situated on a slope. The archaeologist and pilot Eduardo Herran, discovered the Astronaut in 1982.

The Inca

The Inca people are perhaps the most well-known of all the early Andean peoples. This civilization thrived during the 1400s and early 1500s. The Inca carved the mountains into **terraced** farmlands. They grew corn, potatoes, squash, tomatoes, peanuts, chili peppers, coca, cassava, and cotton. They raised guinea pigs, ducks, llamas, alpacas, and dogs. They made their clothing out of llama wool and cotton. Their houses were made from stone or adobe mud. Practically every man was a farmer, who grew his own food and made his own clothing. They built long roads through the mountains from Ecuador to Chile with tunnels and bridges. Two of these roads were over 2,000 miles (3,218 km) long. They also built **aqueducts** to their cities. They united all the people in an area that extended south to Chile and Argentina and north to Colombia. Starting in the 1400s, the Inca ruled over more than 12 million people who spoke 20 or more different languages. Today, millions of people travel to Peru to see the ruins of the Inca city of Machu Picchu, which was an important city in the Inca Empire.

Several huge circular depressions made of terraced land has been found at Moray, an archaeological site in Peru. Archaeologists are not certain what their purpose was, but have found that there is a 27 degree Fahrenheit (15 degree Celsius) temperature difference between the top of the structure to the bottom. It is believed that the Inca may have designed the depressions to study the effect of different climates on growing crops.

City of the Sun

The capital city of the Incan empire was high in the Andes of central Peru. It was called the "City of the Sun." The city, now called Cuzco, still contains much of the Incan architecture. In 1983, UNESCO declared the city a World Heritage Site.

This picture shows the massive stone wall of a fortress in a complex called Sacsayhuaman in Cuzco, Peru, the former capital of the Incan empire.

Today, the city of Cuzco has a population of over 300,000 people.

End of an Empire

The highly organized and stable Inca empire lasted for several centuries. It crumbled, however, once Christopher Columbus landed in the Americas.

The empire ended in approximately 1532. Just a few hundred Spaniards destroyed the empire. They used guns, a weapon that the Inca had never seen or used, to take the empire down.

Living the High Life

Today, about one-third of the entire population of South America lives in the Andes. The cultures and traditions of these people differ from region to region. Most of the people speak Spanish or Portuguese. However, millions of people speak South American Indian languages including Quechua and Aymara. To them, Spanish is a **foreign** language. People in the mountains have bodies that are adapted to life at very high altitudes. They have larger lungs, so they can take in more **oxygen** with each breath. Their red blood cells are larger and can carry more oxygen throughout their bodies. Their hearts are also larger than the hearts of people living at lower elevations. Shepherds in southern Peru live at some of the highest altitudes in the world— 17,000 feet (5,181 m). Most people start to feel **altitude sickness** at or before 10,000 feet (3,048 m).

FAST FACT

Descendants of the Inca make up approximately half of the population of Peru. They speak Quechua. Many farm the land and raise herds of animals.

These children live in the Andes. They are posing with their alpacas.

Sparse Populations

Between Patagonia and the southern limits of the altiplano in Bolivia, the Andes are sparsely populated. A few small groups of shepherds and farmers live on the lower slopes. The most important cities and the largest concentrations of populations are found farther to the north, from Bolivia to Colombia. Quechua-speaking Indians make up roughly half of the population of Bolivia. Other people are Spanish-speaking mestizos. Mestizos are people with mixed heritage. They have both European and Indian **descendants**.

A South American cowboy living in the Pampas or the Patagonian grasslands is sometimes called a gaucho.

The Peruvian village Písac holds a market every Sunday, Tuesday, and Thursday. The market attracts many tourists from the nearby city of Cuzco.

CHAPTER 6
Natural Resources and Tourism

The Andes Mountains are rich in **natural resources** including copper, silver, tin, gold, and other metals. These resources contribute to the economic development of towns and cities within the Andes. Millions of tourists also visit the Andes each year to hike, camp, ski, tour through national parks, and experience the breathtaking views from the mountains.

This person is working on a coffee plantation in South America.

This picture shows an aerial view of an open-pit copper mine in the Atacama Desert in Chile.

Mining Industry

The mining industry of the Andes Mountains is one of the most important in the world. It started shortly after the Spanish arrived in South America in the 1500s. Mining is especially extensive in the southern parts of the Andes. People mine for copper in Chile and Peru, tin in Bolivia, silver, lead, and zinc in Bolivia and Peru, gold in Peru, Ecuador, and Colombia, platinum and emeralds in Colombia, bismuth in Bolivia, vanadium in Peru, and coal and iron in Chile, Peru, and Colombia. There are also several deposits of petroleum along the eastern side of the Andes.

FAST FACT

Bismuth is a silvery-white metal that is highly resistant to heat and electricity. Vanadium is a silvery-white soft metal. It is often combined with steel and iron to make tool steel and cast iron.

Agriculture

Tobacco, cotton, and coffee are the main agricultural export crops grown in the Andes. Tobacco grows best from sea level to about 2,000 feet (610 m). Cotton grows at elevations up to 6,233 feet (1,900 m). Coffee grows best up to about 5,000 feet (1,524 m). Approximately 12 percent of the world's coffee is produced in Colombia and the bulk of Colombian coffee is of high quality. The central and eastern cordilleras produce the best coffee. The country has done an excellent job marketing its coffee through the character named Juan Valdez. This fictional character has appeared in advertisements for the National Federation of Coffee Growers of Colombia since 1959. He is meant to represent the Columbian coffee farmer.

National Parks

Many of South America's most beautiful national parks and wilderness areas are within the Andes Mountains. Millions of tourists visit the parks each year. Torres del Paine National Park in southern Chilean Patagonia includes mountains, a glacier, a lake, and thousands of plant and animal species. A small, but spectacular group of mountains, called the Cordillera del Paine is the park's main feature. Other national parks include Chingaza National Park and Iguaque National Park in Colombia. Bolivia has several national parks that cover more than six million acres (2,428,113 hectares). Ecuador has set aside about 25 million acres (10,117,141 hectares) of its land for national parks and nature reserves.

Torres del Paine National Park is a popular hiking destination in Chile. There are clearly marked paths and breathtaking views for hikers.

In 1959, the Galápagos became Ecuador's first national park, and in 1978 the area was declared a World Heritage Site.

The Galápagos Islands

The Galápagos Islands are a group of islands in the Pacific Ocean. They are part of Ecuador. In 1984, the islands were added to the World Network of Biosphere Reserves under UNESCO's Man and the Biosphere Program. Travelers, scientists, and nature lovers admire and study the islands because many of the plants and animals living there are found only in the Galápagos. For example, the Galápagos giant tortoise is the largest living species of tortoise and is the islands' namesake. It lives only in the Galápagos. The ecosystems on the islands and within the surrounding waters are among the most fragile and unique on Earth, but are constantly threatened by pollution, tourism, and poachers.

The El Tatio Geyser Field is located high in the Chilean Andes. A geyser is a hot spring that periodically erupts and throws water into the air. This area is one of the world's most active geyser regions.

The Top of the World

Thousands of mountaineers visit the Andes every year, but because of the sheer magnitude of the mountain range, many of the peaks remain unclimbed or have only had a few **ascents**. Oddly enough, the highest peak in the Andes, Mount Aconcagua, was one of the first major peaks to be climbed. In 1898, a Swiss climber named Matthias Zurbriggen reached the top of Aconcagua. Today, Aconcagua is one of the most visited mountains in the world. This is partly because the easiest route to the summit does not involve climbing up icy glaciers. However, many climbers ascent too quickly and become very sick with altitude sickness. Many have died from the sickness. Other difficult climbs in the Andes are within Los Glaciares National Park in southern Argentina. Mount Fitz Roy and Cerro Torre are huge peaks that attract the very best mountaineers in the world.

Mount Fitz Roy is located near El Chaltén village in the southern Patagonian ice field in Patagonia, on the border between Argentina and Chile.

A Big Cat

Pumas live within the Torres del Paine National park. These sleek animals are also called cougars, panthers, or mountain lions. They have been seen roaming at elevations as high as 19,000 feet (5,800 m). Pumas are large, muscular animals with sharp claws and teeth. Males are larger than females and can weigh up to 200 pounds (90 kg). The puma has fur that is usually the same color all over its body including on the back, sides, limbs, and the tail. Pumas are active mainly at night or at dusk or dawn. They hunt cattle, sheep, goats, and other animals. They often hide their dead prey by dragging the carcass to a secluded **cache** area and covering it with leaves and **debris**.

NOTABLE QUOTE

*"As a cultural **anthropologist**, I [Johan Reinhard] have spent the greater part of the last 12 years studying high-altitude ceremonial sites in the Andes. During that time I have made more than a hundred ascents above 17,000 feet (5,182 meters), and the more time you spend with a mountain, the more it seems alive."*

—"Sacred Peaks of the Andes," March 1992, *National Geographic* magazine

TIMELINE

200 million years ago	The Nazca plate collides with the South American plate
100 million years ago	The Andes Mountains begins to form
20,000 years ago	Nomads enter North America
10,000 B.C.	People are living in the Andean foothills and valleys
1200 A.D.	The Inca civilization is founded and begins to grow
1400s	The Inca conquer most of the Andes and the civilization thrives
1500s	Mining industry begins in the Andes Mountains
1532	The Spanish conquer the Inca
1898	Swiss mountaineer Matthias Zurbriggen becomes the first European to climb Mount Aconcagua
1911	Machu Picchu is discovered in Peru's Andes
1939	The archaeologist Paul Kosok discovers mysterious shapes made by the ancient Nazca people
1959	The Galápagos Islands become Ecuador's first national park
1973	Peru establishes Manu Biosphere Reserve
1983	Cuzco is declared a World Heritage Site
1985	Nevado del Ruiz erupts and kills more than 23,000 people
2001	A huge burial ground of the Inca is discovered outside Lima, Peru
2002	Conservation International and Peru's National Institute of Natural Resources agree to join forces in an effort to protect a 7.4-million acre (30-million hectare) area of tropical forest spanning two countries

GLOSSARY

adapted Changed so as to fit a new or specific use or situation

agile Able to move quickly and easily

agricultural Relating to cultivating soil, producing crops, and raising livestock

altitude sickness Sickness that is caused by the effects of high altitudes on humans

anthropologist A person who studies human beings especially their physical characteristics, their origins, and their cultures

aqueducts Channels for water, especially ones for carrying large quantities of flowing water

aquifers Rocks that can contain or transmit groundwater

ascent Rising or climbing up

biological diversity The biological variety in an environment as shown by numbers of different species of plants and animals

cache A place or hiding for storing something

carrion Dead or decaying flesh

civilization The way of life of a group of people

climate The long-term weather conditions in an area

colonists People who live in a colony; a colony is an area of land ruled by another country

crust The outer part of Earth

debris Fragments of rock and other materials

depression A shallow hole in the ground

descendants People who come from an ancestor or particular group of ancestors

eco-regions Large areas of land or water containing geographically distinct groups of species, natural communities, and environmental conditions

elevations Heights above sea level

empire A major political unit with a large territory or amount of people under one ruler with total authority

ethnobiologist A person who studies the relationships between people, living things, and environments

foreign Describing something unfamiliar

geometric Relating to geometry, which is the area of math that deals with points, lines, angles, surfaces, and solids

grazing Feeding on growing grass

indigenous Living things that are naturally found in a particular region or environment

insulation Protection that prevents the loss of heat

irrigation system An artificial system that supplies dry land with water

lava Melted rock that comes from a volcano

livestock Animals that are kept or raised by people

molars Teeth with rounded or flattened surfaces that are designed for grinding

natural resources Materials found in nature that are valuable or useful to humans

nomads People who have no permanent homes and move from place to place

oasis A fertile spot in a desert

oxygen A colorless, tasteless, odorless gas, which forms about 21 percent of the atmosphere and is necessary for life on Earth

pinnate Resembling a feather

plateaus Flat areas of high land

plate tectonics A scientific theory that describes Earth as being composed of gigantic moving plates

pristine Fresh and clean

raids Sudden attacks or invasions

rain shadow A dry area on the side of a mountainous area that is sheltered by the wind and precipitation

resplendently Shining brilliantly

sacred Describing something that is deserving of respect or honor

temperate Describing a climate that is usually mild without extremely cold or extremely hot temperatures

terraced Horizontal ridges made in a hillside to conserve moisture and prevent loss of soil for agriculture

INDEX

FIND OUT MORE

BOOKS

Blue, Rose and Naden, Corinne. *Andes Mountains (Wonders of the World)*. Raintree, 1995.

Maynard, Charles W. *The Andes (Great Mountain Ranges of the World)*. Powerkids Press, 2004.

Wilson, Jason. *The Andes (Landscapes of Imagination)*. Oxford University Press, 2009.

Richardson, Hazel. *Life in Ancient South America (Peoples of the Ancient World)*. Crabtree Publishing, 2005.

WEBSITES

WWF—Northern Andean Montane Forests
http://wwf.panda.org/about_our_earth/eco regions/northandean_montane_forests.cfm

UNESCO: Historic Sanctuary of Machu Picchu
http://whc.unesco.org/en/list/274

Lake Titicaca
www.laketiticaca.org/

National Geographic: Andes Expedition
www.nationalgeographic.com/features/ 97/andes/